Secret Societies

© Aladdin Books Ltd 1996

Designed and produced by
Aladdin Books Ltd
28 Percy Street
London W1P 0LD

First published in
the United States in 1996 by
Copper Beech Books,
an imprint of
The Millbrook Press
Brookfield, Connecticut 06804

Editor
Jim Pipe
Design
David West Children's Book Design
Designer
Flick Killerby
Picture Research
Brooks Krikler Research
Illustrators
Francesca D'Ottavi, Lorenzo Cecchi,
Lorenzo Pieri, Susanna Addario, Claudia
Saraceni – McRae Books, Florence, Italy

Printed in Belgium

Library of Congress Cataloging-in-Publication Data
Ross, Stewart.
Secret societies / by Stewart Ross : illustrated by McRae Books.
p. cm. — (Fact or fiction)
Includes index.
Summary: A look at secret cults, covering everything from
Ninjas to Mafia gangs, codes, signs and symbols, and strange
ceremonies.
ISBN 0-7613-0533-5 (lib. bdg) — ISBN 0-7613-0510-6 (pbk.)
1. Secret societies—History—Juvenile literature. 2. Secret
societies—Juvenile literature. [1. Secret societies.] I. McRae
Books. II. Title. III. Series: Ross, Stewart. Fact or fiction.
HS125.R67 1996   96-24579
366—dc20   CIP AC

FACT *or* FICTION:

Secret Societies

Written by *Stewart Ross*
Illustrated by *McRae Books, Italy*

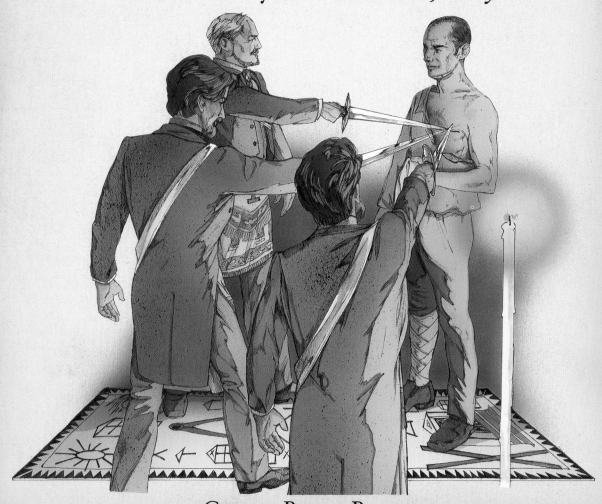

COPPER BEECH BOOKS
BROOKFIELD, CONNECTICUT

CONTENTS

INTRODUCTION

The world is not what it seems to be...

The suspicious-looking man leaving a suitcase at the railroad station – could it be a bomb? Who are the people that meet once a week in the house whose curtains are always closed? Graffiti painted on a wall – just vandalism or a coded message?

To which secret society do the respectable men who greet each other with strange handshakes belong? The group sitting in a dark corner of a nightclub – a football club committee or a drug cartel?

There have always been men and women with secret lives. Many were quite harmless, just members of private or outlawed groups. They did not see themselves as misfits but as the wise or chosen few.

Others kept their activities secret for more sinister reasons. They were the ruthless villains of the dark underworld of crime. Some were fanatics, others were driven by greed or fear. All were dangerous.

So as you enter the shadowy realms of secret societies, remember that the innocent and the wicked are not easily distinguished...

You Have Been Warned!

REBELS AND OUTCASTS

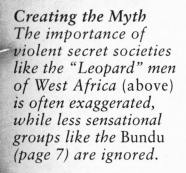

There have always been outsiders and there always will be. And when there are outsiders, they will band together in secret.

There are two types of secret groups. One is made up of people who join together for their own comfort or protection. Often, like the early Christians, they share an unpopular or banned religious belief, and they are forced to become secret to protect the safety of their members. But all they really want is to be left in peace, and once their views are accepted by society, there is no need for them to remain secret.

Other groups are aggressive. They are formed for strength in the fight against society and its laws. Many of these are criminal gangs, such as the Mafia, or political or religious fanatics, such as the Assassins.

Creating the Myth
The importance of violent secret societies like the "Leopard" men of West Africa (above) *is often exaggerated, while less sensational groups like the* Bundu *(page 7) are ignored.*

IT'S GOOD TO BELONG
We all like to belong. Because of this, people sharing the same interests join together for mutual support. Some groups are more secret than others.

Some of the early British trade unions were forced to meet in secret because in the 19th century their activities were illegal. But the Masons organization, formed to help its members, has secret meetings (*left*) out of choice.

Less secret is the banding together of groups like truck drivers and magicians, who also use their own rituals and language.

DEATH IN THE DARK. The hooded killer, the hidden cache of arms, the stealthy assassin – many of the most deadly secret societies have been military groups, determined to get their way by murder and mayhem.

But when history is clouded by myth and legend; as with the Japanese ninja clans of the 11th to 16th centuries A.D., it is hard to tell fact from fiction (*right*).

CRIMINAL CANCER

Organized crime has spread like cancer through all societies. Its means: violence. Its end: wealth. Its cover: secrecy.

The streets of ancient Rome were invaded with rival crooks. In 19th-century Europe, thieves and pickpockets banded together to outwit the police and rob the rich in the sprawling cities of the Industrial Revolution. Today, all around the world, gangs run every kind of racket.

These Russian gangsters are happy to pose for the camera (*right*) – a far cry from the slick professionals in books and films.

In a World of Their Own
In many secret societies, members shut out the opinions of people outside the group. Militia members in Michigan (left), see themselves as law-abiding defenders of American ideals, even though most outsiders regard them as dangerous, racist fanatics.

THE POWER OF PERSONALITY

Religious cults, such as the Moonies (followers of Reverend Sun Myung Moon), often rely on the charisma and forceful personalities of their leaders. They prey on people who are unhappy with their lives or who are easily led by others.

Secret Learning
In the African country of Sierra Leone, secret societies known as Bundu *are just a part of daily life.*

Boys and girls go to them to learn about local traditions and customs.

THE FANTASY WORLD OF CRIME. Films and books often portray criminal gang members as colorful people who lead exciting lives (like these villains in the film *Dick Tracy, above*).

But real gang members are often just mindless thugs who use violence and terror to destroy the lives of innocent people.

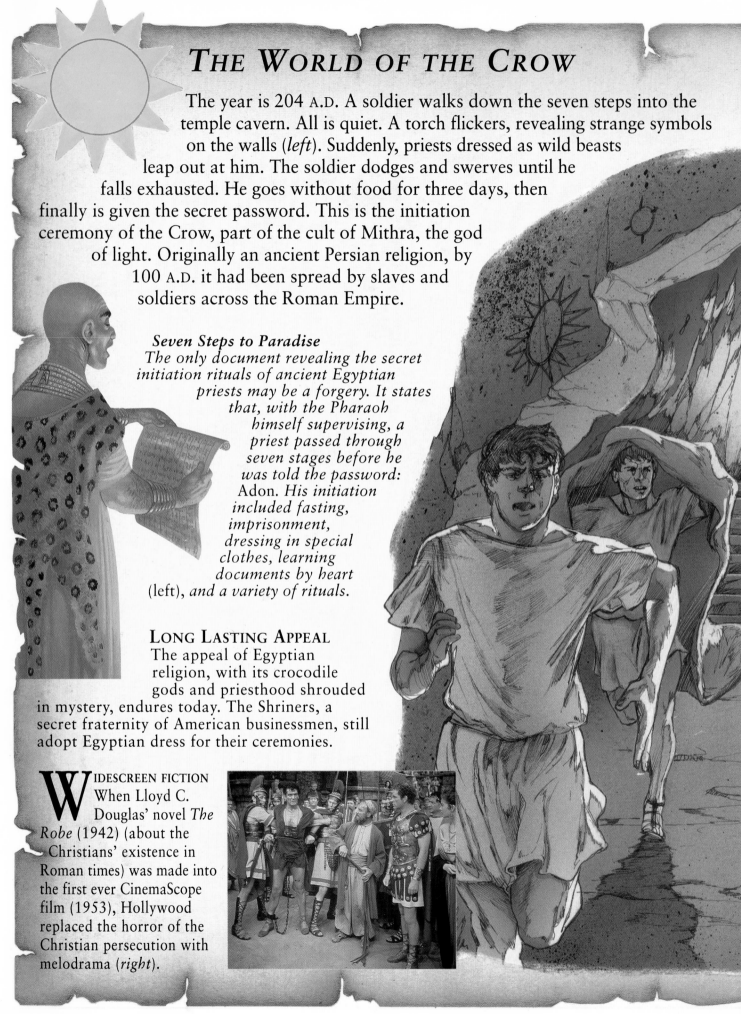

THE WORLD OF THE CROW

The year is 204 A.D. A soldier walks down the seven steps into the temple cavern. All is quiet. A torch flickers, revealing strange symbols on the walls (*left*). Suddenly, priests dressed as wild beasts leap out at him. The soldier dodges and swerves until he falls exhausted. He goes without food for three days, then finally is given the secret password. This is the initiation ceremony of the Crow, part of the cult of Mithra, the god of light. Originally an ancient Persian religion, by 100 A.D. it had been spread by slaves and soldiers across the Roman Empire.

Seven Steps to Paradise
The only document revealing the secret initiation rituals of ancient Egyptian priests may be a forgery. It states that, with the Pharaoh himself supervising, a priest passed through seven stages before he was told the password: Adon. His initiation included fasting, imprisonment, dressing in special clothes, learning documents by heart (left), and a variety of rituals.

LONG LASTING APPEAL
The appeal of Egyptian religion, with its crocodile gods and priesthood shrouded in mystery, endures today. The Shriners, a secret fraternity of American businessmen, still adopt Egyptian dress for their ceremonies.

WIDESCREEN FICTION When Lloyd C. Douglas' novel *The Robe* (1942) (about the Christians' existence in Roman times) was made into the first ever CinemaScope film (1953), Hollywood replaced the horror of the Christian persecution with melodrama (*right*).

Running from Demons (below)
A soldier flees from wild beasts and demons during the rites that make him a member of the cult of Mithra.

THE ANCIENT MYSTERIES

Many ancient Greeks joined secret cults because they promised their members the key to happiness in the afterlife.

The most famous cult was at Eleusis. It was dedicated to Demeter, the goddess of agriculture who was influential in the underworld. All Greek-speaking people could join. The initiation ceremony (*right*), still a mystery today, took place in the fall.

A DANGEROUS CEREMONY

Until 300 A.D., the all-male cult of Mithra (*right*) was one of the main religions competing with Christianity in Europe.

One of its rites involved mock combat with soldiers in a dark cave. But when the Roman Emperor Commodus was initiated, he accidentally killed another member.

The Dark Side
The violence of Mithra is shown in this evil-looking deity (left) *from about 190 A.D.*

SEBASTIAN'S SECRET. The Romans knew all about the mythical power of secret societies. Under Emperor Diocletian, Christianity was outlawed and went underground.

Sebastian, a Christian officer in the imperial guard, was discovered to be a Christian, and was therefore sentenced to death.

When Sebastian's body was pierced with arrows (*right*), St. Castulus healed the wounds. Furious, Diocletian had Sebastian beaten to death with cudgels.

OBEDIENT TO DEATH

Syria, 1092 A.D. High on the walls of his mountain castle, Hassan-ben-Sabbah takes his visitor by the arm and points to a guard on a distant turret.

"You see that man?"

"I do."

"Then watch!" Hassan signals with his hand. Immediately, the guard salutes, steps forward and falls to his death on the jagged rocks below.

The visitor shivers.

"That," Hassan explains, "is my power as master of the Assassins. All my followers would do the same."

Seal of Death
Assassins knew before they opened an order what it might contain. This sign, pressed into the wax of the seal while still soft, meant only one thing: a command to assassinate.

SHIITE FANATICS
When the prophet Muhammad died in 632 A.D. (*left*), Islam was left without a leader. One group, the Sunnis, claimed that any Muslim could lead the movement. Others, the Shiite, said that only the descendants of Muhammad could rule.

In time, the Sunnis came to power and the Shiites went underground. The Assassins were a fanatical Shiite sect, dedicated to fighting the Sunnis.

THE GRIM REALITY. The world of the hired killer continues to fascinate moviegoers. But the glamorous film assassin (*right*) bears no relation to the real assassins – who see cold-blooded murder as just a job.

HIGH AND MIGHTY

Hassan-ben-Sabbah founded the Assassins at the end of the 11th century. He demanded total obedience, and like so many cult leaders, promised a place in paradise in return. He even built a beautiful garden (*below*) to trick drugged followers into thinking they could see heaven. The name "Assassin" comes from the killers' practice of drugging themselves with hashish.

THE RUBAIYAT

The Shiite author of *The Rubaiyat of Omar Khayyam (1859)*, translated into English (*left*) by Edward FitzGerald (1859), studied with Hassan, founder of the Assassins. But neither the Assassins' behavior nor the Rubaiyat's praise of alcohol were part of traditional Islamic teaching.

Loyal Leap (main picture)
On an order from his leader Hassan, the Old Man of the Mountain, an Assassin guard throws himself from the battlements of Alamut castle.

THE ISMAILIS

The Assassin sect died out in the 14th century. But the Ismailis, led by the Aga Khan, have taken on some Assassin features, particularly their insistence on obedience to the leader.

In 1866, the then Aga Khan claimed he was descended in direct line from the fourth Grand Master of Alamut to win a $15,000 tribute from a group known as the Khojas. Today the Aga Khan (*above right*) is as famous as a racehorse owner as a religious leader.

SHADOW WARRIORS

Japanese Ninja warriors – "the invisible ones" – belonged to the deadliest secret societies of all. Each ninja clan had its favored weapons and secret skills, specializing in silent movement and bodily control. A trained ninja could slow his pulse and breathing and remain still for days.

During the Age of Strife (16th century), ninja clans worked for warlords (*left*) who battled for control of Japan. One ninja was sent to kill a rival general, Uesugi Kenshin, who was guarded day and night. Undaunted, the assassin entered his castle and hid for days in the cesspit below a toilet. Finally, the victim appeared – and the ninja struck (*right*).

MASTERS OF DISGUISE

Though they are usually shown dressed in black, most ninja spent a lot of their time in disguise – in an attack on Kaminojo Castle in 1592, for example, they dressed as castle guards.

Hidden Weapons

Ninjas often dressed as priests (right), *hiding a variety of deadly weapons beneath flowing robes.*

The more expert could disguise themselves as dancers – or even female musicians (below right), *using their flute as a club in times of emergency!*

FANTASY WAR. Before the 1970s, the ninja were little known outside Asia. Today it is unusual to find anyone who has *not* heard of them. This is due mainly to the popularity of video and computer games in which good and bad ninja fight beside monsters and superpeople in the endless Battle of the Levels (*above*)!

Samurai's Sixth Sense

The ninjas' most deadly foes were Japan's knights, the Samurai (right). *The Samurai's sharpest skill was* zanshin, *the ability to feel the presence of danger, even when it could not be seen or heard.*

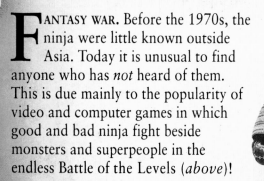

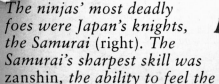

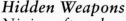

THE IKKO-IKKI

Not all Japanese secret societies relied on stealth. In the 15th century, a monk from the Buddhist Jodo sect unified other sects into a group known as the Ikko-ikki (Single-Minded League). Their members were told that death in battle would grant them a place in heaven.

For fifty years the Ikko-ikki army threatened to capture the emperor in Kyoto. But once the general Uesugi Kenshin had been killed, Oda Nobunaga was able to crush the sect.

THE PERFECT HERO. Once the cowboy was the hero of the comic book. Then it was the spaceman, battling with aliens. Now the sword-swinging, wall-climbing ninja warrior leads the fight against crime. Nothing done by the original ninja can compare with the fictional valor of their comic-strip contemporaries (*top*).

CREATING THE NINJA MYTH

From the 17th century onward a series of Japanese writers invented the ninja myth. They gave the ninja magical powers and dreamed up crazy James Bond-style machines, such as shoes for walking on water (*right*), amazing underwater breathing gear, and a flame-throwing tank disguised as a cow!

One writer said the classic ninja costume was not completely black but had a hint of red, so that if a ninja was wounded his blood would not show and he would seem invincible.

Look before You Leak
Some historians believe that the ninja who assassinated Uesugi Kenshin was sent by Kenshin's arch rival, Oda Nobunaga.

PIZZA POWER. Many of the original ninja were cold-blooded murderers. Time has softened their image, however.

Today, fictional ninja are seen as firmly on the side of right – even when they are pizza-scoffing turtles (*right*, from the film *Teenage Mutant Ninja Turtles*, 1990).

THE FALL OF THE TEMPLARS

In 1307, the attention of bankrupt King Philip IV "the Fair" of France was drawn to the Templar Knights, a group of crusaders founded to recover the Holy Land from the Muslims.

The Templars (whose seal is shown *left*) were now rich and powerful. They vowed obedience to their commander, held secret ceremonies and were rumored to have associated with the Assassins. Heresy! cried King Philip. The Templars were rounded up, tortured, and their order dissolved – and all because King Philip wanted their money.

Fiction Mightier than Fact
Hundreds of Templar knights were burned at the stake (left) after denying a range of false charges made by King Philip. These included spitting on the holy cross, worshiping cats, and secretly killing members who tried to leave the Order.

SECRECY – OR DEATH
In medieval Europe any group meeting in secret might be suspected of heresy (having opinions different from church teachings). Suspicion of heresy could bring in the dreaded Inquisition, set up by Pope Gregory IX in 1231 to force heretics to change their beliefs. Many suspects were tortured. Those who refused to change their beliefs were burned at the stake. Understandably, many genuine heretics kept their beliefs as secret as possible.

The Witches' Coven
Medieval villagers feared no secret society more than the witches' coven. In the dead of night, when the moon was full, witches (left) were said to meet with the devil in a ritual of dance and wicked ceremony. How do we know? Because many poor souls confessed to witchcraft, often under torture.

GRAIL GUARDIANS. The Holy Grail, the cup which Jesus Christ was supposed to have used at his Last Supper, inspired medieval legend – and modern film. In *Indiana Jones and the Holy Grail* (*above*), the Grail is guarded both by an immortal Templar knight and by a secret sect distinguished by a red cross tattooed on their chests.

FAITH IN THE SHADOWS
John Wycliffe (c.1330–1384, *above*) was an English religious reformer whose Lollard followers were forced by harsh heresy laws to keep their beliefs and meetings secret. The movement survived for over a century.

The Chosen Few?
The Gnostics were a secret cult, not because they feared persecution, but because they wanted to keep their secret route to God to themselves. There were both Christian and Muslim Gnostics. The extreme members of the cult believed in dark magical powers.

The Sign of the "Great Secret"

KING OF THE BEGGARS

Seeing a well-dressed young man approach, the beggar slips a piece of soap into his mouth and chews. Foam froths over his lips. As his prey gets closer, he starts to groan. The man shakes his head sadly and throws him a couple of coins. When he is out of sight, the beggar spits out the soap and picks up the coins. He keeps one and puts the other aside as tax for the Grand Coesre, or "King of Beggars," the head of a 15th-century criminal empire of French conmen.

PIGGY IN THE MIDDLE

The Grand Coesre, based in Paris, used all sorts of tricks to cheat people. *Marcandiers* pretended to be merchants who had been robbed, *Francs-Mitoux* pretended to have fainting fits in public, and *Malingreux* made themselves look as if they had dreadful swellings and sores.

An even more remarkable deception was the Italian man who dressed himself up as one of Siena's six pigs trained to eat up garbage. In this disguise, he stole flour and corn from the marketplace while prowling around on his hands and knees!

Weird Words
Like many secret groups, French criminals (right) developed a language of their own. Some words (e.g. "lyans" for arms) were taken from French. Others, such as "chourin" for a knife, were of gypsy origin.

GREEK SECRETS

Greece fell to the Muslim Turks in the 15th century. In time, secret groups of Greeks, the *klephts*, took to the hills and kept up a constant challenge to the conquerors' rule. They gathered into tribes, each with its own rituals. Today, they are remembered as much for their stirring campfire poetry recitals (*left*) as for their military exploits.

Cruel Tricks
In a world of almost constant famines, plagues, and wars, the false beggars (above) deprived thousands of genuinely needy people of charity.

THE VEHM AND THE VIRGIN

Medieval Westphalia (now part of Germany) was a lawless place – until the Holy Vehm appeared. The Vehm was a secret organization dedicated to destroying evil. It had its own courts and particularly unpleasant punishments.

Those found guilty of a serious crime were ordered to kiss a huge bronze statue of the Virgin Mary. As they approached, the statue opened to reveal an interior covered with spikes. A special mechanism drew the offender inside and the doors slowly closed (*right*)...

B RAVEHEART. Like the *klephts*, the Scots led by William Wallace carried on the fight against their country's invaders in secret. The death of King Alexander III (1286) had left Scotland vulnerable to the ambitions of its English neighbors. Within ten years Scotland had, in theory, ceased to exist. But led by William Wallace (1274–1305), the Scots fought back – sometimes in the open, often waging guerrilla warfare. Wallace's life was made into the film *Braveheart* (*above*) in 1995.

THE SHELL SYNDICATE

The Coquillards ("shell people") organized the underworld of 15th-century Dijon, France, with ruthless efficiency.

As well as banditry, assassination, and con tricks, the followers of the mysterious King of Coquille were famous for their ability to pick the locks of "coffers, chests, and treasuries" (*right*).

SECRET SIGNS AND SYMBOLS

Secret societies need ways of communicating that cannot be understood by outsiders. The simplest is a means of recognition, such as the Masons' handshake. There are also simple messages, such as "All clear," that can be given without speech.

Most groups in society develop their own vocabulary, some of which eventually becomes part of standard language. London cockneys have a rhyming slang, saying "dog and bone" for "telephone," truck drivers say "hammer" for "accelerator," computer users "surf" the internet, while criminals and many youth and minority cultures also use their own private slang. More sophisticated groups devise signs, symbols, and even codes.

Homage to Kali
By clasping his hands together, a Thug said to other members of his gang: "Homage to the goddess Kali" – a salute that no one outside the cult would recognize.

An Innocent Scratch
The art of using the Thug hand signals was to make them seem part of everyday movement.
Innocently scratching your chin, for example, could be a call for a private meeting, while a hand held across the chest, pointing downward gave the order to kill. Some of the main signs are shown on the right.

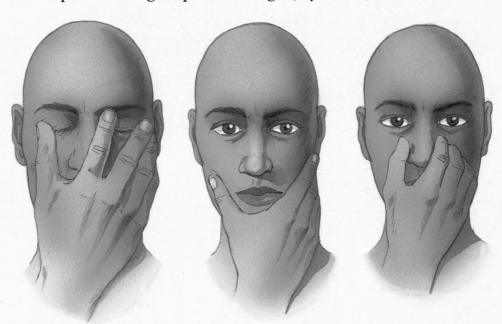

DON'T ATTACK • LET'S TALK IN PRIVATE • TONIGHT

MYSTIC MOONLIGHT
The symbols used by secret societies were always more than just attractive patterns.
Their designs contained hidden meanings. The Illuminated Ones used a crescent moon, symbolizing light. Other societies made up seals marked with a range of symbols, such as a bull for power, a tree for life, the sea for time, and a flower for peace.

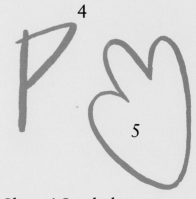

Mithra Symbols
1. Concentration. 2. Important meeting. 3. Official seal.

Skoptsi Symbols
4. Danger signal.
5. Member's house.

CODES AND CIPHERS

Spies and governments usually pass secret messages in code. They use the normal letters of the alphabet arranged in different patterns and orders. Many secret societies, however, prefer ciphers. A cipher uses an entirely new alphabet. Its advantage is that it is not always recognized as writing.

Three examples of secret ciphers are shown here – but true to the nature of the societies themselves, no one is exactly sure to which society each cipher belongs!

A B C D	E F G H	I K L M
○	☾	☿
○ ○₁○₂○₃	☾ ☾₁☾₂☾₃	☿ ☿₁☿₂☿₃
N O P Q	R S T U	V X Y Z
♀	♃	♂
♀ ♀₁♀₂♀₃	♃ ♃₁♃₂♃₃	♂ ♂₁♂₂♂₃

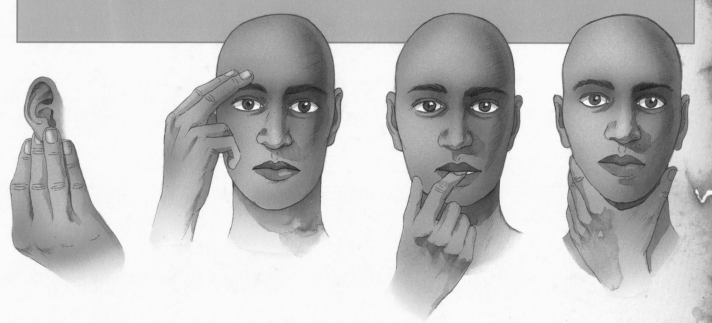

ALL CLEAR • I AM A PRIEST • I AM A MEMBER • BE SILENT

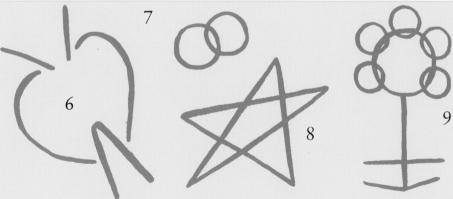

Assassins
6. *Badge of order.* 7. *Chief's symbol.*
8. *Initiate's mark.*

Sufi Emblem
9. *Meaning of life tree.*

EVERYDAY SIGNALS

All societies, secret or not, have signals and codes that show that the individual belongs to and follows the rules of the society.

For example, the army salute shows that the soldier obeys the superior, while bowing in Japan and handshakes in the West are signs of mutual respect.

HUNTED PRIESTS

At dawn the priest catchers seized a maid and forced her to open the castle gates. Terrified, the girl shouted a warning to her mistress. The noise woke Father Blount and his servant and they hurried into the secret priest hole.

They remained for ten days in this cramped space, while the house (*top*) was ransacked. Eventually the hunters took an evening off. The Roman Catholic priest and his servant crept from the castle under cover of darkness. Blount swam the moat, while his companion tricked the guards into opening the gates. By morning the pair were well on their way to London.

WHY SO SECRET?

In the past, people with unpopular religious beliefs were forced to go underground. Often, they were then falsely accused of carrying out terrible rituals and criminal acts. But in modern countries where there is freedom of religion, we should be wary of any cults that still feel the need to hold secret meetings.

Blount's Bolt (main picture)
Scotney Castle, Kent, 1592.
The Roman Catholic priest
Father Blount swims
across the castle moat
to escape the clutches
of the priest catchers.

SHINING TROUBLE MAKERS

The Illuminated Ones first appeared in the mountains of 16th-century Afghanistan (*above*). In the beginning they were a mysterious sect claiming knowledge of a secret doctrine handed down from the prophet Muhammad (their symbol is shown *left*).

In time, they developed elaborate rituals and spread to other countries, where they were said to be involved in all kinds of troublemaking.

HIDE AND SEEK

Roman Catholic priests were barred from the England of Elizabeth I (1558–1603). Nevertheless, many entered the country from the continent and found shelter in the country houses of the great Catholic families. Here special hiding places, known as "priest holes" (*right*), were made for them. Some of the priest holes made by the master carpenter Nicholas Owen had two entrances and a toilet!

TESTIS OVAT

LIE-POWER

During the reign of King Charles II (1660–1685), Titus Oates stirred up suspicion by proclaiming that a group of Catholics were plotting to kill the king and take over the country. The so-called Popish Plot (1678) – which never existed – led to the execution of 35 innocent people. In time the public became suspicious and Oates was flogged and jailed (*left*).

THE ROSICRUCIANS. The believers in the works of Christian Rosenkreuz ("rosy cross") are one of Europe's most fascinating secret societies. It began when the *General Reformation of the World*, supposedly written by Rosenkreuz 200 years earlier, was published in 1614.

The book combined magical science, Christianity, and the occult to produce an intriguing mystery. Cult members claimed they felt no hunger, they could command spirits, and could make themselves invisible. But to this day no one knows if the whole society was just a big hoax.

THE FREEMASONS

Vienna's Freyhaustheater, September 30, 1791. At 7:00 P.M. Wolfgang Amadeus Mozart steps forward to conduct *The Magic Flute*, his new opera. As the capacity crowd falls silent, the overture begins.

After a few dramatic bars, the music melts into a gentler theme. Then the orchestra plays a surprising knocking rhythm. A few members of the audience glance knowingly at each other: Mozart is a member of Europe's most famous secret society, the Freemasons, and he has incorporated the secret Masonic knocking rhythm into his opera (*below*)!

THE RISE OF THE MASONS

Freemasonry is one of the largest fraternal organizations in the world. It claims to encourage brotherhood and moral behavior among its members. Based on medieval guilds of stonemasons it grew into a set of social societies, called lodges, with secret rituals (*top*). Colonists brought the organization to America, where some historians believe it played a key part in the American Revolution.

Boards and Aprons
The aprons worn at Masonic rituals (above) *derive from those worn by stonemasons to protect their clothes. Also central to Masonic rituals are tracing boards, which originated with the plain wooden boards on which masons mixed their mortar. During a ritual the board is placed on the ground and stood on by the participants* (right).

Roll Up, Roll Up!
Chest bared, trouser-leg rolled up, and with swords pointing to his heart, a recruit goes through the elaborate and secret ritual required of all those joining a Lodge of Freemasons.

Such ceremonies originated with the first Grand Lodge, set up in 1717.

Helping Hands
Although membership is secret and limited to men over the age of 21, many prominent people – Duke Ellington (*right*), Peter Sellers, Wolfgang Amadeus Mozart, and at least twelve American presidents – are known to have been Masons. Freemasons have been criticized for secretly favoring fellow members in employment or government.

Finger Signals
Masons keep the exact details of their famous handshake a secret, but it involves gripping a person's hand and pressing four times with the thumb in certain places (left).

The handshake enables Masons to recognize each other without saying a word.

S ACRED SYMBOL. In Rudyard Kipling's story, *The Man Who Would Be King* (1898), two English conmen journey to a remote part of central Asia. When the Masonic sign around John's neck matches their holy symbol, the local people think he is a long-lost god-king (*above*). But power soon goes to his head – with disastrous results.

HOLY MUTILATION

Perhaps the strangest secret society were the 19th-century Skoptsi – God's Chosen Ones – a fanatical Russian sect famous for their wealth and the willing castration of their members.

The Skoptsi took the Orthodox Church's view that priests should not marry to bizarre lengths – they thought the only way to reach a godlike state was by removing their sexual parts! Given the extreme (and irreversible) nature of its rituals, the cult was remarkably popular. Among its powerful followers were the Tsarina and the Tsar's personal advisor.

Members Only
The "three M" mark (left) *indicated a new member of the secret Russian Skoptsi sect.*

A MIX OF OLD AND NEW

The Skoptsi mixed ideas from the old mystery religions with those of the Russian Orthodox Church (*below*), which had broken from the Roman Catholics in 1448. By the mid-19th century, the sect had bases in most Russian provinces. Tsar Nicolas I sent hundreds of Skoptsi to live in Siberia in an attempt to halt the spread of their ideas.

But because the wealthy sect gave large sums to government officials and the church, it was very hard to stamp out.

Blood Money (below)
When the Russian police searched the cellars of a house in Morchansk (1869), they found a small fortune in gold, jewels, and banknotes. The wealth was to be used by the fanatical Skoptsi to further their political ambitions.

THE DAILY FLAIL

The Skoptsi started in the mid-18th century among the deviant members of the Sect of Flagellants, or Khlysty. Since medieval times this sect had used whipping for public punishment (see page 24, *far left*).

The most famous Khlysty of the modern era was the charismatic holy man Grigory Yefimovich Rasputin (1872–1916), who was murdered by Russian aristocrats because of his almost hypnotic influence over the Russian royal family.

Sacrificial Murder
Thuggee – practiced by the Indian Thugs – was an extreme way of worshiping the terrible goddess Kali. Members of the secret sect sacrificed human beings to the goddess by killing them by strangulation or poison (so as not to spill blood). The practice was outlawed by the British in the 1820s.

Terrible Kali
Devi, the greatest of the Hindu goddesses, has two forms: kindness and fierceness. As Kali "the black," goddess of destruction, she is shown standing on the body of her partner Shiva with a necklace of skulls and severed arms hanging from her waist. Two of her four arms hold emblems of death, while the other two carry symbols of blessing.

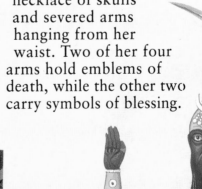

CRIME SCHOOL

"We hung about in the shadows, watching the gentlemen walking by. After ten minutes, Joe nudged me and pointed to an elderly man across the road. Joe sauntered across to check out his prey. Seconds later, he was back. 'Yeah! Silk handkerchief. Go on!'

"Shaking like a leaf, I moved up beside the man and slipped my hand into his pocket. The handkerchief came out as easy as anything. That evening we sold it for sixpence. I felt great – the richest man in the world!" Another young London pickpocket had learned his trade.

But though life may have felt sweet for this young crook, it was often very short in the brutal, gang-dominated underworld of Victorian London.

OLIVER! Charles Dickens' novel *Oliver Twist* (1837–1839) describes the criminal underworld of 19th-century London with brutal frankness. When the book was turned into the musical *Oliver!* (*right*), however, Fagin's gang of young thugs became a school of sweet little boys.

HARSH TRAINING

Most real-life Fagins were cruel men with no time for failure – less clever boys were beaten soundly. Once caught, many of the boys were forced into work houses where rough tasks ruined the sense of touch needed for picking pockets.

A Hard Pair
Gangland London was filled with nice characters. When asked to pay for his meal, hardened criminal Jimmy Spinks (left) plunged the sandwich shop cat into the fryer. Dodger Mullins (right) got rid of an unwanted girlfriend by shoving her from a moving car.

Apprentice to Crime
London's fashionable Covent Garden, 1841. While his mates keep watch, a young pickpocket makes his first theft. In an age when many children were forced to work long hours in dangerous jobs, pickpocketing seemed an easy option.

Siege Snooper (above)
*In 1911, Winston Churchill
ordered the breakup of a gang of
Russian anarchists on Sidney Street,
London, who were thought to be
planning a bomb attack.*

WIDES VS MUGS

British films of the 1930s show a
sleepy, innocent world. But several
of London's slum areas were run by
criminal gangs who saw only two
types of people: "Wides" (criminals)
and "Mugs" (potential victims). The
police entered gang territory only
with great care and sometimes
fought street battles with villains.

TWIN TERRORS. The 1960s British
crime scene was dominated by
Ronnie and Reggie Kray – the
flashy but vicious Kray twins. Although
involved in all kinds of criminal activity,
including murder, the pair were strangely
popular. Their lives were made into a
film in 1990 (*below*). But the safe streets
of the Kray era are a myth – their gang
organized violence rather than removed it.

THE BLACK HAND STRIKES

On June 28, 1914, Archduke Franz Ferdinand of Austria (*left*) and his wife Sophie arrived in the Bosnian capital, Sarajevo, for a state visit. After a failed terrorist attack, their route was altered. This confused their driver and at 10:45 A.M. he took a wrong turn down a side street. Realizing his mistake, he began to back up. Too late.

Nineteen-year-old Gavrilo Princip stepped forward and fired two shots at point-blank range. Within minutes, the Archduke and his wife were dead. The Serbian Black Hand – sworn enemies of Austria – had struck. The assassination sparked off a chain of events that led to World War I.

SECRET POLITICS. History is dotted with political groups working in secret. Some, like the Chinese Boxers, the Black Hand, and the Italian Carbonari, plotted to remove foreign powers from their homeland.

Others, like the Russian anarchists (page 27), wanted to end "government persecution and hunger" everywhere – but their bloody tactics won them few supporters.

BOXING THE BARBARIANS

Encouraged by the Dowager empress Tzu Hsi, in 1900 a secret society of Chinese nationalists, known as the Righteous and Harmony Fists, or Boxers, attacked Western (barbarian) embassies in Beijing and slaughtered fellow citizens who had converted to Christianity. Several Triad gangs (page 36) supported the Boxers (whose flag is shown *above left*).

Spirit of Rebellion
The Boxer rebellion (right) *was defeated by a combined European army, but its spirit encouraged anti-imperial feeling which led to the successful Chinese Revolution of 1911.*

BURNING FOR FREEDOM

When Emperor Napoléon conquered Italy and made the Frenchman Joachim Murat king of Naples, the Carbonari society – "charcoal burners" – was formed to drive him out. After the fall of Napoléon, the Carbonari worked to unite the Italian states under a single government.

CARBONARI SYMBOLS

The Carbonari used symbols to show new members what their aims were:
• *Tree*: the breadth of the movement, its quest for equality and strength • *White sheet*: the movement's purity • *Salt*: a preservative
• *Water*: cleansing from vice
• *Crown of Thorns*: a warning
• *The Cross*: suffering for the cause
• *Ladder*: gradual, steady progress
• *Bundle of Sticks*: working together
• *Ribbons*: faith • *Pickax*: to pierce the body of the enemy
• *Furnace*: to burn the body of the enemy • *Shovel*: to scatter the enemy's ashes

PHANTOM PLOTTERS. Soviet dictator Joseph Stalin was convinced that everyone around him was part of a secret plot. So on his orders millions of innocent people were sent to work in camps. The awful conditions in the camps were the subject of Alexander Solzhenitsyn's novel *One Day in the Life of Ivan Denisovich* (1962, filmed in 1971, *below*).

Assassin Gavrilo Princip, (above) a member of the Serbian nationalist Black Hand gang, is led away by police after the assassination.

THEY SEEK HIM HERE... Baroness Orczy's romantic novel *The Scarlet Pimpernel* tells of a secret society of young Englishmen, the League of the Scarlet Pimpernel, who rescue citizens from the French Revolution's Reign of Terror (1793).

THE FICTIONAL UNDERWORLD

The two men meet high on a footpath above a gaping chasm. Without warning, one of them lunges forward and grasps the other in a wrestling hold.

For a few seconds they sway together. The more agile man slips free. His assailant screams and waves his arms frantically, then disappears from sight. Peering over the cliff, Sherlock Holmes watches his enemy rebound off a rock and disappear into "that dreadful cauldron" of foaming water (*main picture*). So dies Professor Moriarty, the deadliest criminal of his generation – in the fictional world at least, the evil gang leader is always defeated by the forces of good.

Good and Bad
In contrast to the adult world, many children's gangs (like the seven kids who search for One-Eyed Willie's treasure in The Goonies, *above) are on the side of right.*

Others, of course, are not so pleasant – who wants to spend time with Danny's enemies in the musical Grease!

KID'S GANGS. As playground gangs loom large in children's real lives, so fictional gangs are featured widely in their stories. From the pirates in *Treasure Island* and the *Huckleberry Finn* gang to Enid Blyton's *Famous Five* (*left*) and the Hyenas in *The Lion King*, children's films and literature are bursting with secret bands.

Lord of the Flies
In William Golding's famous novel The Lord of the Flies, *a group of schoolboys are stranded on a tropical island after an air crash. They soon return to a primitive state, forming rival gangs. One gang forms its own rituals – chanting and dances –* (below) *connected with hunting and feeding.*

"MR. BOND, IT IS TIME FOR US TO SAY GOODBYE." So says James Bond's evil opponent, unaware that 007 will always find a way to escape the horrible death he has prepared for him. Bond's enemies have included gang leaders Dr. No, Hugo Drax and Goldfinger and vicious henchmen such as the metal-toothed Jaws, the hat-slinging Odd Job, and Rosa Klebb with her poison-spiked shoes.

Pussy Galore
James Bond's greatest enemy has always been the international crime organization called SPECTRE. We rarely see the face of its leader Blofelt, but we always know him by the white cat he loves to stroke (left)!

THE NAPOLÉON OF CRIME

Sir Arthur Conan Doyle's infamous Professor Moriarty, Sherlock Holmes' toughest opponent, was fiction's first "superbrain" criminal. Called the "Napoléon of crime" by Holmes, Moriarty ran a criminal network based in London. In their last encounter, Holmes and the professor wrestled high above a gorge into which – apparently – they both fell to their deaths. The public outcry at Holmes' deathwas so great, however, that Conan Doyle was forced to bring his detective back to life in *Return of Sherlock Holmes* (1905).

THE ORIENTAL MORIARTY. When English writer Sax Rohmer (Arthur Ward) wrote *Dr. Fu Manchu* in 1913, little did he realize that he had created one of the most popular fictional villains of all time.

The sinister Chinese genius, who returned in *Reenter Fu Manchu* and in the Christopher Lee film *The Face of Fu Manchu*, has become even more famous than his European counterpart, Professor Moriarty.

HAPPY VALENTINE'S DAY

To the ordinary citizens of Chicago, February 14, 1929 was a normal, happy St. Valentine's Day – a time of love and laughter.

But the Al Capone mob were no ordinary citizens. The city's most feared gangsters had chosen this day to get even with their old enemies, the Bugsy Moran gang. In Capone language "getting even" meant murder.

Using police uniforms as disguises, Al Capone's boys cornered their rivals in a side street. Together with a dentist and a garage mechanic who happened to be passing by, Bugsy's mobsters were lined up against a wall and machine-gunned to death.

Gangster myths. The plentiful supply of cheap machine guns turned some large U.S. cities into battlefields. The enduring image of the age is the violin case (*left*) being used to hide a machine gun, but few gangsters would have bothered with such a deception.

Films show gangsters like Capone (*top*) being treated as celebrities. This is partly true – far from living his life in secret, Capone did ride in his limousine to the theater. But he wasn't popular – just so powerful that few dared to oppose him.

Bugsy malone Nothing turns fact into fiction quicker or more easily than this musical. Take the cruel and brutal Chicago of Al Capone, make the characters children, add a few catchy songs, swap machine guns for foam guns... and create one of the most popular musical shows of all time (made into a film in 1976, *above*).

BOOZE BUCKS

During Prohibition, U.S. government agents seized and destroyed (*left*) huge quantities of illegal beer and spirits. But alcohol was always available.

The trade was in the hands of secret criminal gangs – bootleggers – who oversaw the illegal production (*below*), distribution, smuggling, and sale of all types of liquor.

As the underground industry involved millions of dollars, the police were often too scared to act – or took bribes to turn a blind eye. In 1929, 60 percent of the Chicago police force were said to be corrupt.

Tea for Two?
In a fit of moral fervor, the U.S. government banned the production and sale of alcohol in 1919. After 13 years of law breaking on a massive scale, the Prohibition crusade was dropped in 1933.

Say It with Lead
To safeguard their criminal activities, on February 14, 1929, Chicago's Al Capone gang wiped out seven rivals in a single shooting.

THE UNTOUCHABLES

"This is a war to the finish!" declared Chicago Police Commissioner William F. Russell when he learned of the Valentine's Day Massacre (see page 32). But despite numerous publicity triumphs (*main picture*), Elliot Ness (*left*) and his team of "Untouchables" in fact did little to hurt the empire of Al "Scarface" Capone. The only charge that could be made against him was carrying a concealed weapon. Within a year the uncrowned king of Chicago was free.

Then the FBI worked on the one area where they knew Capone was vulnerable: tax evasion. In June 1931, he was arrested again. This time, Capone was charged with thousands of offenses and finally sent to prison for 11 years. Russell's war was won.

INTERNATIONAL CRIMEBUSTERS

International gangs require an international police force – Interpol (International Criminal Police Organization, *right*) – to hunt them down.

Founded in 1923, Interpol coordinates the work of national police forces and holds a bank of information for their use. It is particularly active in the fight against terrorism and drug trafficking.

Lucky Escape
Extradition is the surrender of an alleged criminal by one authority to another (left). *But when train robber Ronald Biggs fled to Brazil in 1965, the Brazilian government refused to extradite him because his girlfriend was pregnant.*

RETURN OF THE PINK PANTHER. When the witless Inspector Clouseau (Peter Sellers, *right*) sets out after a criminal gang, the trail is bound to become a chaotic streak of destruction. This is the plot of *The Revenge of the Pink Panther* (1978), in which Sellers doubles as a godfather figure of the Italian-American Mafia.

In the real world, it takes teams of agents years of painstaking work to bring gang leaders to trial – and even then there is no certainty that the charges will stick.

THREE

final edition

TH

GANGSTER LEADER CAPTURED IN DAWN RAID BY ELLIOT NESS AND HIS MEN

STATE SECRECY

Individual states tend to be more concerned with enforcing their own laws than those of the federal government. To combat this, in 1908 the Federal Bureau of Investigation (FBI, *left*) was set up to investigate breaches of federal law. The Central Intelligence Agency (CIA) emerged forty years later to handle international security. With wide-ranging powers and secret operations, the CIA often appears more like a secret society than a government agency.

ZERO TO HERO. *The Mask* is the latest in a long tradition of anti-gangster films. When the hero, played by Jim Carrey, wears an ancient mask with magical powers, all his wishes come true – bad news for the villains!

Chicago Daily

February 1931 - forty-eight pages

UNTOUCHABLES

The Untouchables

Elliot Ness and his FBI team, known as "the Untouchables" because they were thought to be above bribery, have been immortalized on the silver screen (below). But Ness' real triumph was not over Al Capone – but police corruption.

Cosa Nostra

Thousands of heavily-armed troops patrolled the streets, while armored vehicles guarded key points and helicopters and aircraft roared overhead. Surprisingly, the military were not on maneuver but guarding the most famous trial in Italian history. After years of painstaking and dangerous investigation, 474 people had been brought to a heavily-defended courthouse in Palermo, Sicily and accused of crimes organized by the Mafia, the world's most famous criminal society. The defendants were kept locked up in an iron cage throughout the trial (*below*). Two years later, 338 were found guilty.

It is 1986, and for the first time in history, the power of the Mafia had been seriously challenged.

The Mafioso

The word *Mafia* may have come from an Arabic word that means "place of refuge." One of the meanings of the word describes the confident style of behavior of the Mafioso, a man of great importance in the community.

The Mafioso gains power by exploiting people who have no where else to turn – for once he has carried out a favor for them, they are forever in his debt.

Terror Tactics

The first Mafia gang began in 13th-century Sicily as a secret society (left) that used violence to get its own way. Later, other gangs formed to oppose Spanish rule of the island. By the 1800s, the gangs dominated Sicily.

Their members follow a secret code of honor, known as Omertà, *which forbids telling the police about crimes.*

MAY I BURN...

Joining the Mafia involves a famous ritual. The recruit pricks a finger and lets blood drop (*right*) onto a picture of the Virgin Mary and the baby Jesus. The image is then burned. Taking the ashes in their hand (*left*), the recruit swears, "If I fail... may I burn and be turned to ashes like the ashes of the Image."

THE GODFATHER. Novelist Mario Puzo wrote *The Godfather* in 1969. Three years later his story of how Sicilian immigrant Don Corleone and his family built up a criminal network backed by force and violence, was made into a film (*left*).

One of the Godfather's real-life counterparts was Charles "Lucky" Luciano (*bottom*). Arriving in the United States in 1906, Lucky built up a criminal empire of drug-peddling, prostitution, and protection. He acquired his nickname by avoiding arrest until 1936. Released ten years later, he was deported to Naples where he died in 1962. His body was returned to New York for an elaborate funeral (*below*).

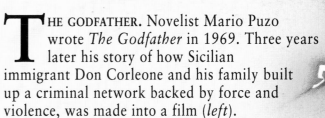

A RUTHLESS EMPIRE

In 1891, law enforcement agencies first noted the existence of an American Mafia, known as *Cosa Nostra* or "Our family." By the 1920s, Italian Americans had come to control most organized crime in the United States.

Today, the U.S. Mafia's 6,000 or so members are arranged in a loose network of regional gangs called *families*. The families take in an estimated $70 billion each year from gambling, prostitution, drug trafficking, and extortion.

The U.S. Mafia ruthlessly protects its worldwide empire. Those who investigate its activities are often the target of threats and assassinations.

TEA MONEY

London, March 1994. A note is shoved under a restaurant door. The owner, Kan, knows that a triad request for "investment" means pay up – or else. But when a group of men come for their "tea money," Kan refuses and they leave – angry. A week later, unexplained fights break out between customers – regulars understand and stay away. Then come the threatening phone calls: If Kan doesn't pay he will be "chopped" with cleavers. As a warning, the gang beats up Kan with iron bars. Kan pays up.

Triad Terror Tactics (main picture)
When Kan refused to "invest" in Triad protection, the gang trashed his restaurant. The police estimate that six out of 10 Chinese businessmen in England pay Triad protection money.

CRIMINAL CEREMONY
Because it began as a sect, the rituals and symbols of the Chinese Triad organization are more elaborate than those of most criminal groups. For initiation ceremonies members wear traditional dress (*top*) and carry the triangular pennant from which the organization got its name.

The Not-So-Secret Society
The Japanese Yakuza has an estimated 90,000 members in 3,000 gangs. But many of their activities are not secret – they even advertise for members. In 1992, when laws were passed to control them, thousands of members took to the streets in protest (above).

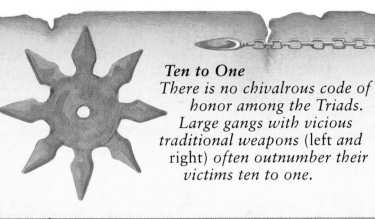

Ten to One
There is no chivalrous code of honor among the Triads. Large gangs with vicious traditional weapons (left and right) often outnumber their victims ten to one.

ANCIENT VILLAINY

The Triads are the oldest criminal secret society in the world, beginning in 36 A.D. as a Chinese Buddhist cult. In the 1820s, they joined patriotic movements under the banner: Expel the (foreign) Qing dynasty, restore the (Chinese) Mings (*below*). But their real aim was to build a criminal empire.

The different Triad gangs are only loosely connected and often fight each other. Many members join while they are at school because they are being bullied. But few realize that once they become involved, there is no escape from this evil, violent world.

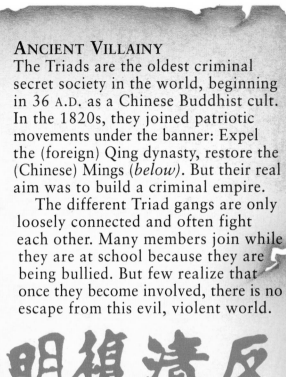

POLITICAL TERROR

Twentieth-century urban life is painfully vulnerable to the bomb-carrying terrorist. By simply threatening violence, comparatively small and ill-funded secret societies, such as the anti-British Irish Republican Army (IRA) or the Palestinian Hamas (*below*), exert tremendous influence.

Hamas suicide missions, such as killing 25 people on a bus in Jerusalem in 1996, seriously threatened the Palestinian-Israeli peace talks.

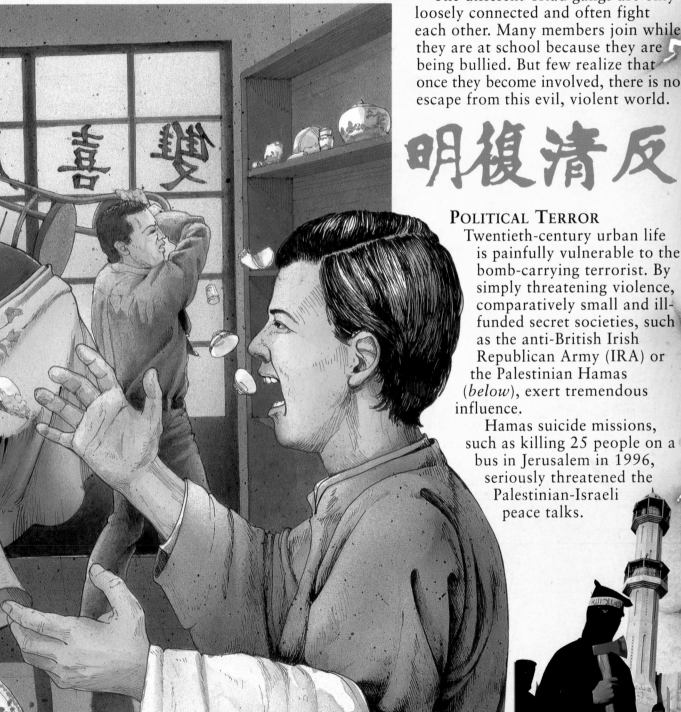

THE DEADLY TRADE

The police had been watching the building for weeks. They videotaped everyone who used it, eavesdropped with long-range directional microphones, and tapped its phone lines. Finally, when they had all the evidence they needed, they struck.

Armed officers smashed through the back door. Taken completely by surprise, the gang had no time to hide the bags of white powder piled on the floor of a first-floor room. Two men surrendered at once. A third drew a gun and fired wildly at the advancing police. A single shot from a marksman sent him reeling to the floor. Another ring of deadly drug smugglers had been broken.

Bust Up (main picture)
The police raid the headquarters of a gang of drug smugglers. But the men arrested are small-time. The drug barons who control the vile trade make sure that the trail freezes over long before it gets to them.

KINGS OF COCAINE
With an estimated income of over $2 billion per year, the Colombian cocaine barons of the 1980s Medellin Cartel (such as Pablo Escobar, *left*) were among the richest people in the world. Their wealth made them almost impossible to bring to justice. Those who threatened them – from local police to government ministers – were killed or bribed into silence.

The Drug Wars
In the 1980s the U.S. federal government waged a "war on drugs," partly in an effort to reduce the power of the cartels (gangs) that became so powerful through money earned from drug trafficking.
Government forces destroyed many of the small refineries where the drugs were processed (above) – but unfortunately did little to reduce the power of the cartels.

Arty Markers
To the ordinary person they look like bits of harmless – even attractive – graffiti.

But those in the know realize that some of the elaborate wall paintings are really a gang's way of marking out its territory. They state quite clearly, "This is our patch. Keep Out!"

THE GROWING BROTHERHOOD

Since World War II, Mafia-style gangs have spread worldwide. Among the best known are the Asian and Turkish Mafias and the Jamaican Yardies, with annual takings of around $600 million. They are tied in a love-hate relationship, cooperating in drug smuggling but fighting when their interests overlap.

The Russians Are Coming
The most distressing development in recent years has been the growth of the Russian Mafia (one of the most powerful Russian "godfathers," Oleg Chichkanov, is shown above).

It lies behind a massive crime-wave sweeping Western Europe, stealing items such as cars and computers and smuggling them back to Eastern European countries.

Bond meets the mob. The Russian Mafia appeared in the latest James Bond film *Goldeneye*, where Robbie Coltrane plays (*above*) a shady Russian gang leader. But his wisecracking character is far too jolly to be involved in the real mafia, where murder is just part of business.

THE POWER OF RITUAL

All societies, secret or otherwise, use rituals, especially for initiation. Their many purposes include:
(1) providing a shared experience that gives members a common identity; (2) defining what the society is all about; (3) testing a recruit's sincerity, perhaps by demanding that they do something unpleasant or difficult; (4) building up a sense of tradition; (5) providing a public sense of purpose that makes leaving the group more difficult.

Most rituals, like conventional religious services, use special clothes, music, isolation, abstinence, tests, renaming, special food or drink, and the repetition of special phrases.

HOLLY HIGHS

Native American tribes had a variety of elaborate coming-of-age ceremonies. The *huskenaw* ceremony was designed to make young men obedient to their elders.

The men were locked in a dark hut for three weeks while they were lectured on their responsibilities and given holly leaves (*top*) and bark to chew (*right*). This gave them hallucinations (believed to be insights into another world) that prepared them for entry into the world of adulthood.

Native American secret societies revolved around rebirth: At each rebirth a member reached a higher level in the society. Some tribes used "sweat lodges." A frame of willow, covered with hides, was erected over a fire. Water was poured over the logs to create a dark, steamy "sauna" (below).

THE KEY TO THE DOOR

In the West today, apart from close-knit religious groups such as Jews, the ritual associated with coming-of-age (or reaching the age of legal maturity, usually 18 or 21) is generally just a party or large family meal.

Its most common symbol is a key, indicating that the young person now carries the key to their own life.

One of Us (main picture)
A gang of biker thieves watches as a new member hands over his first batch of stolen goods to the leader.

This ritual proves to the others the new member is worthy of joining, and gives him a sense of belonging to the gang.

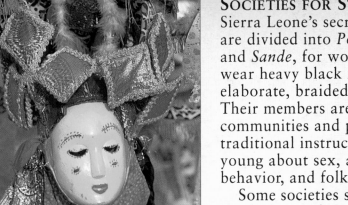

SOCIETIES FOR STABILITY

Sierra Leone's secret societies are divided into *Poro*, for men, and *Sande*, for women, who wear heavy black masks with elaborate, braided hair (*left*). Their members are in almost all communities and provide traditional instruction to the young about sex, adult behavior, and folk knowledge.

Some societies specialize in particular professions, such as medicine, psychiatry, and even dancing and conjuring.

HOODED TERROR

Formed in the South following the Northern victory in the Civil War, the Ku Klux Klan opposed civil rights for black people, murdering dozens and persecuting thousands in a campaign of violence.

In the 20th century, the secret racist society added Jews, Catholics, and Communists to its list of enemies.

The KKK's emblem is the burning cross. At ritual ceremonies hooded members (*above*) carry huge flaming crosses to a meeting place and arrange them in a fiery circle on the ground.

SECRET STUDIES. Student associations at universities known as fraternities and sororities also hold semi-serious initiation ceremonies. The student societies, whose names are made up of letters of the Greek alphabet, are derived from associations once common in ancient Athens. In the 1978 film *National Lampoon's Animal House* (*right*), rival fraternities battle on campus.

YOU WILL OBEY!

U.S. Congressman Leo J. Ryan was disturbed by reports from Guyana. Ex-Methodist minister Reverend Jim Jones had emigrated there to establish his People's Temple sect. But were his followers being treated properly? And were they free to come and go as they wanted? Ryan went to investigate. He never returned. Near his murdered corpse investigators found almost a thousand other bodies, the poisoned remains of Reverend Jones' followers. After supervising his "act of revolutionary suicide," the minister had finally shot himself.

SCIENCE FICTION?
Outsiders are deeply suspicious of the way the Church of Scientology (founded by Ron Hubbard in 1954) controls its members. This hasn't stopped such stars as Tom Cruise and John Travolta (*top*) from joining.

Mass Madness
On the orders of their leader, Reverend Jim Jones, members of his People's Temple line up for a fatal drink of Kool-Aid laced with cyanide. The 1978 tragedy killed 914 people – probably the largest mass suicide in history. Cut off from the outside world, members could not imagine life without their cult.

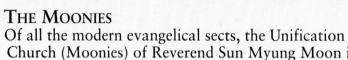

THE MOONIES
Of all the modern evangelical sects, the Unification Church (Moonies) of Reverend Sun Myung Moon is perhaps the most famous. The Korean industrialist founded his part-Christian, part-Taoist church in 1954. Since then it has spread around the world. The central ritual of the Moonies is marriage (*above*). Partners are chosen and blessed by Reverend Moon, who is criticized for the tight hold he keeps over his followers.

DANGEROUS OR JUST MAD?

How can those on the trail of dangerous secret societies distinguish the innocent from the villainous? What, for example, do they make of the Order of the Peacock Angel? Dressed in robes emblazoned with the image of the peacock, male and female cultists work themselves up into a frenzy by dancing before a giant statue of their sacred bird.

SECT BUSTING

Waco, Texas, 1993. Members of a fanatical religious sect the Branch Davidians, wanted for firearms offenses, barricaded themselves in their compound. The law decided to meet force with force and layed siege to the compound. Weeks later, the sect chose death over surrender and its compound erupted in a ball of fire. Why? Because in the unstable world of the cult, a fanatical leader can persuade his followers to do almost anything.

Militia Groups

The U.S. constitution gives every citizen the right to bear arms. Faced with soaring crime, successive administrations tried to limit this right. In April 1995, a secret citizen militia group, tired of what it saw as government interference, detonated a bomb in Oklahoma City. Once again, the world was reminded that if a society operates in secret, it probably has something to hide.

THE DANGERS OF SECRECY

Secrecy can be exciting – being part of a group that perhaps few know about or belong to – but it is often dangerous.

Many of the secret societies in this book used secrecy as a weapon – to force members to follow the demands of the leader and to make it difficult to leave.

Religious sects say their secrecy is to protect some special knowledge that will give their members a place in heaven – but it is usually a way for the leader to exploit his followers. Finally, the criminal society promises "protection" or easy money – but at what cost in human lives?

SECRET WORDS

Anarchist Someone whose ideal society does not have any form of government.

Argot Slang, originally made up by thieves.

Assassin Originally a follower of the Old Man of the Mountains, a member of a fanatical 11–13th century military order in Persia and Syria notorious for secret murders (*left*). Today the word is used to describe any secret political murderer.

Bundu The secret societies of the west African country Sierra Leone.

Cartel A political or economic group that has ganged up to kill the competition (in more ways than one). Often used to describe the powerful drug gangs of South America.

Castration Removal of the testicles.

Cipher A secret code using symbols instead of the letters of the alphabet.

Cult A system of beliefs, often extreme in nature. Also means the followers of these beliefs.

Fraternity A society formed on the basis of brotherhood (i.e. only male members). The female equivalent is known as a sorority.

Freemasonry Originally a guild or union of stonemasons, but formed in the 18th century into a secret fraternity. The Masons unite in lodges as a kind of social club and to help each other out.

Heresy Beliefs that go against those of the established religion or authorized teaching. Believers are known as heretics.

Kali The Hindu goddess of destruction (*left*), worshiped by the Thug cult in India.

Loan-sharking Lending money to people at such high rates of interest that the interest is soon worth more than the original debt. Often backed up by force.

Lodge The meeting place of some societies, and for the Freemasons, the name of a branch of the society.

Mafia Originally the spirit of opposition to the law in Sicily, but later a secret criminal organization that started in Sicily and spread to the rest of the world, particularly the United States.

Mithra The Persian sun god (*above left*), whose worship became popular in the Roman Empire.

Ninja A member of one of the clans of trained assassins in medieval and early modern Japan.

Protection Racket A system of demanding money from storekeepers or restaurant owners in return for not damaging their property.

Sect A group of followers, often used to describe small or extreme religious groups.

Templars Members of a religious and military order (*above left*), the Knights of the Temple.

Terrorist Someone who belongs to a group that tries to achieve its political aims by violent means.

Thug A member of an Indian religious fraternity of murderers. Today the word also means anyone who behaves violently.

Triad One of the various Chinese criminal secret societies (*right*), also known as the Dark Society in Chinese. Named after the use of the triangle in their rituals.

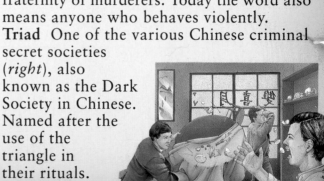

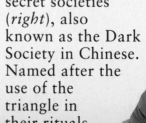

SECRET SOCIETIES' TIMELINE

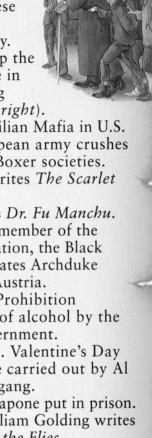

c.2000 B.C. Secret initiation rituals widespread in Egypt.

600 B.C. Start of the Mysteries in ancient Greece.

0–100 A.D. Cult of Mithra spreads across Roman Empire (*left*).

36 A.D. Triads begin as a Buddhist Cult.

64–313 AD Christians persecuted in the Roman Empire.

11th century–13th century Assassins at their most powerful in Syria and Persia.

11th–16th centuries Ninja clans active in feudal Japan (*bottom of page*).

13th century First Mafia activities in Sicily.

1231 Pope Gregory IX sets up Inquisition to hunt out heretics in Europe.

1274–1305 William Wallace organizes patriotic resistance to English invaders of Scotland.

1307 King Philip IV of France disbands the Templar Knights, burning hundreds at the stake.

15th century Coquillards organize the criminal underworld in Dijon, France. The King of the Beggars runs a national network of conmen from Paris, France.

15th century Holy Vehm terrorizes medieval Germany.

15th century The Ottoman Turks conquer Greece. The Greek klephts flee into the hills where they form secret societies.

1614 Roman Catholic priest Father Blount escapes from Protestant priest catchers at Scotney Castle, Kent.

1614 Christian Rosenkreuz publishes *General Reformation of the World*.

1717 Freemasons in Great Britain set up Grand Lodge (*above*).

Late 18th century Thugs at their most powerful in India.

19th century The Russian Skoptsi recruit thousands of members to their cult.

1820s Italian Carbonari active.

1820s Triads join Chinese patriotic organizations fighting the Qing dynasty.

1829 Robert Peel sets up the first modern police force in an attempt to fight rising crime in London (*above right*).

1890s–1920s Rise of Sicilian Mafia in U.S.

1900 A combined European army crushes a revolt by the Chinese Boxer societies.

1905 Baroness Orczy writes *The Scarlet Pimpernel*.

1913 Sax Rohmer writes *Dr. Fu Manchu*.

1914 Gavrilo Princip, a member of the Serbian terrorist organization, the Black Hand, assassinates Archduke Ferdinand of Austria.

1919-1933 Prohibition (banning) of alcohol by the U.S. government.

1929 St. Valentine's Day massacre carried out by Al Capone's gang.

1931 Al Capone put in prison.

1954 William Golding writes *Lord of the Flies*.

1960s London gangland dominated by Krays.

1978 913 members of the People's Temple cult commit mass suicide in Guyana.

1986 338 Mafia members found guilty in Palermo, Sicily.

1980s War against drugs conducted by U.S. security forces, aimed largely at drug cartels operating in Central and South America.

1990s Rise of Russian Mafia following the breakup of the former Soviet Union (*below*).

1993 FBI siege of a religious cult in Waco, Texas ends in deaths of over 50 cult members.

1995 Bombing of Oklahoma City by members of an extreme U.S. militia group.

INDEX

Photo credits *Abbreviations: t – top, m – middle, b – bottom, l – left, r – right.*
Cover & 36–37 – Paramount courtesy Kobal. 4-5, 10br, 11 ml, 21, 22t, 24t, 27t & 33m – Mary Evans Picture Library. 6m, 7m, 10br, 11mr, 12m, 17, 20b, 22b, 30t, 34m, 35t & b, 36b, 38, 39, 40m & b, 44t & b, 45 – Frank Spooner Pictures; 6b – Canon courtesy Kobal. 6-7, 7t, 15t, 23t, 34b & 41m – Rex Features. 7b & 43t – The Hutchison Library. 8 – 20th century Fox courtesy Kobal. 9t & 14m – Bridgeman Art Library. 9b, 12t & b, 28m & b – AKG London. 13t & 35m – New Line courtesy Kobal. 15m, 16m, 26t, 28t, 33t & 38 – Hulton Getty Collection. 16t – Ancient Art & Architecture. 20t – Stewart Ross. 23b – Allied Artists courtesy Kobal. 26m, 32t & b – Ronald Grant Archive. 27b – Fugitive Features courtesy Kobal, photograph by Blanshard. 29m – Leontes/Norsk Group courtesy Kobal. 29b – Archers/London Films/British Lion courtesy Kobal. 30bl & 41b – Eon/United Artists courtesy Kobal. 30br – Castlerock/Colombia Pictures courtesy Kobal. 31 – Hammer Films courtesy Kobal. 41b – Universal courtesy Kobal.